IPY Agency LLC
1000 Parkwood Circle SE.
Suite 900
Atlanta, GA 30339

Copyright © 2025
Adrienne Alexander

All rights reserved. No part of this book may be reproduced in any form or by any electronic or mechanical means, including information storage and retrieval systems, without permission in writing from the publisher, except by reviewers, who may quote brief passages in a review.

ISBN 979-8-9884620-6-4

The Great PR Heist:
How Public Perception Stole the Truth About Public Relations

www.adriennedalexander.com

The Great PR Heist: How Public Perception Stole the Truth About Public Relations

by

Adrienne Alexander

Table of Contents

Chapter One: The Spin Doctor's Oath 3

Chapter Two: Smoke, Mirrors & Manipulation 9

Chapter Three: The Puppet Masters 17

Chapter Four: Crisis Junkies & Scandal Wranglers 24

Chapter Five: The Strategy Syndicate 33

Chapter Six: The Relationship Hustle 39

Chapter Seven: The Brand Whisperers 45

Chapter Eight: The Digital Detectives 51

Chapter Nine: The Anti-Pr Pr Movement 58

Chapter Ten: When Pr Fails 64

Chapter Eleven: The Comeback Code 70

Chapter Twelve: The Finale 75

To my husband, the man who taught me patience and reminded me often not to get in the ring with everyone. I Love You.

To My Children and Grandchildren, may this one be the one that sticks.

To everyone who believes in me and listens to every idea I get excited about, thank you for every conversation, for every piece of advice, and for being a rock star.

Chapter One

THE SPIN DOCTOR'S OATH

"PR people lie for a living." That's what they say. They say we twist the truth. We distract, deflect, and manipulate. But here's what they never say: "We called our publicist before we called our lawyer." "Our publicist helped us stay out of the news entirely." "Without PR, nobody would've even known our story." That's because that's what PR does, and they rarely make headlines.

They call us spin doctors, shiny-suited illusionists, puppeteers pulling strings behind the scenes. And somehow, after 100+ years of practicing a legitimate communications discipline, that's still the headline. Let's go ahead and set the record straight:
We don't lie. We clarify.
We don't hide. We highlight.
We don't manipulate. We manage meaning.

You have to go back to the beginning to understand why PR has such a complicated reputation. Public Relations was born out of propaganda. The earliest practitioners were marketers, war strategists, and power brokers who used messaging to influence public opinion during wartime. And it worked, sometimes too well. People began to see PR as manipulation wrapped in a mission. Then came advertising. Then came media empires. Then came Hollywood. The public watched celebrities get in trouble, and as a result, they magically became even more famous. They saw politicians embroiled in scandal only to emerge rebranded with the help of a "communications team." And every time someone gave a polished speech, dodged a question, or shifted a narrative, people whispered the same thing, "That's PR."

Except, not always, what they saw was often damage control. What they didn't see was the person behind the scenes saying, "Don't do that."

What They Think PR Is	What It Actually Is
Lying to the public	Strategic messaging rooted in truth
Spinning a story	Reframing with clarity and context
Apology crafting and cover-ups	Crisis navigation, stakeholder comms, brand repair
Making people "look good"	Helping people and brands show up well
Controlling the media	Building relationships that earn visibility

So yes, PR has an image problem. But here's the kicker: we're the ones who fix image problems, and it's time we fix our own.

Let's talk about what doesn't get seen. PR is:

- Spending two weeks crafting a story before a product launch.
- Rewriting a press release four times to fit a journalist's style.
- Coaching clients through a live interview so they don't "uhh" and "umm" themselves out of credibility.
- Anticipating a potential backlash and redirecting the message before it even starts.

We don't work in the spotlight; we work for the spotlight. Not everyone is ready for it, but everyone wants it.

Years ago, a potential client approached me with a business announcement: they were introducing a new product. Beautiful branding. Great backstory. They wanted PR support, press coverage, features, and influencer buzz; the works.

I dug in and asked a few questions.

And it unraveled fast.

The product wasn't ready. The reviews weren't real. The testimonials were "placeholders."

And when I pushed back, they said, "It's fine. We just need to get people talking. You'll figure out how to spin it."

I walked away.

Because here's the thing: I don't spin. I shape. I don't fake stories. I amplify real ones. I won't build momentum around a message I know can't hold. So, where did the lie about lying begin?

Pop culture played a role. Scandal. Ray Donovan. Mad Men. Even Entourage.

Each one gave us the same PR stereotype: slick, shady, untouchable. But the real problem? A few bad actors did lie. Some publicists made promises they couldn't keep. Some chased vanity instead of value. Some let their egos write checks their skillsets couldn't cash. And clients, understandably, left burned, bitter, and ready to blog.

The myth wasn't entirely made up; It just wasn't all true. Here's what the loudest voices forget: the best PR doesn't make noise. It makes it clear. It's the statement crafted before your apology. The brand message makes someone say, "That's so me." It's the journalist callback you got because of a relationship someone like me built ten years ago. Most of our work is unseen, uncredited, and absolutely essential. And let me tell you, nobody becomes a great publicist by accident.

You have to know the media, the people, the timing, tone, language, optics, ethics, and ego, all while juggling a news cycle that resets every 30 minutes.

If publicists had a Hippocratic-style pledge, which we do, the Public Relations Society of America (PRSA) outlines a clear Code of Ethics that includes:

- Advocacy: Serving the public interest by acting as responsible advocates.
- Honesty: Adhering to the highest standards of accuracy and truth.
- Loyalty: Being faithful to clients while honoring the public trust.
- Fairness: Respecting all opinions and supporting the right of free expression.
- But if we had an oath, a ride-or-die, hand-on-heart manifesto, it would sound like this:
- I will tell the truth, even when it's inconvenient.
- I will never promise coverage; I can't deliver.
- I will protect your message as if it were my own.
- I will prepare you for the spotlight, not push you into it.
- I will not lie for you. But I will stand with you.

That's not spin. That's a standard. And the best in this field live by it. Let's be honest. Clickbait gets clicks. Scandal gets attention. Viral outrage drives engagement. And in a world trained to react, PR has become the scapegoat for every carefully worded statement that doesn't sound raw and unfiltered.

But here's what most people forget: raw doesn't always mean real, and loud doesn't always mean right. Sometimes, the most truthful, powerful messages are quiet, careful, and precise. And those messages don't trend because they do their job so well that no one even notices. Publicists don't manufacture truth; we make it land.

At its core, public relations is about connection.

It's about helping people, brands, and movements present themselves in ways that foster trust, loyalty, and lasting relationships with the public. And if that feels revolutionary, it's because we've let the wrong people write the narrative for too long.

"PR Ain't Free, but it's worth it." That's a derivative of the book I wrote in 2020, called Public Relations Ain't Free: And Other Tall Tales Regarding Public Relations, which remains true today. This isn't about clearing our name. It's about reclaiming our power.

We live in a culture driven by clicks that rewards controversy and scandal. If your apology goes viral, your campaign sparks outrage, and your rebrand gets roasted, now people care. Now you're "in the news." But real PR? The kind that's strategic, slow, story-centered, and honest? It rarely goes viral. It's too real for the algorithm. That's why this book exists: to tell the truth louder, show you what PR is, and give this industry back to the people doing the work right.

Chapter Two

SMOKE, MIRRORS & MANIPULATION

"PR is not about hiding the truth. It's about helping people understand it."

People don't trust PR simply because they don't understand it. They see the polished quote and assume there's a cover-up. They watch the press conference and think, "That's scripted." They read the company statement and roll their eyes at the word "transparent" because the average person has repeatedly been taught that if it's packaged well, it must be fake; that if it sounds too good, it probably is. And that "public relations" is code for "professional deception."

But here's the part they miss: PR isn't the reason people don't trust what they're hearing; PR is why the message was worth hearing. When you say "PR," most people picture one of two things: a cover-up or a stunt. They think of the celebrity's apology after the scandal, the politician's press secretary dodging questions, and the corporate spokesperson using thirty words to say nothing at all. And yes, sometimes PR is called in to clean up a mess. But guess what? Most of us would rather help you prevent the fire than spin the flames. Good publicists would rather spend three months helping you build trust than three hours helping you fake a rebrand.

The best PR isn't reactive; It's proactive. It doesn't hide the truth. It helps shape it clearly so it resonates with the people who need to hear it most. But let's get into the meat of it. One of the biggest myths about PR, one that keeps getting recycled in memes, headlines, and side-eye glances at networking events, is this: PR is smoke and mirrors. It's the idea that everything we do is a trick.

A distraction, a game of optics designed to pull attention away from the truth rather than illuminate it. It's why so many people treat publicists like they're peddling fiction, not facts. The irony? People often claim they want transparency, but they don't always recognize it when they see it. We've confused storytelling with lying and message discipline with manipulation.

Let me be clear: there's a difference. Real PR professionals don't deal in deception. We deal in design. We design how a message sounds, how it's received, where it lands, and how it lives in people's minds. We build perception, yes, but perception rooted in truth is one of the most powerful assets a brand or individual can own.

Now, let me say this: manipulation does exist in the field. Some publicists overpromise, spin too hard, or push a false narrative for the sake of buzz. And just as in politics, media, or finance, there are bad players. But those people aren't representative of the field. They're just the ones who make the headlines. And that's precisely how PR got its bad rap.

Let's break it down: manipulation hides or distorts the truth, uses pressure and fear, is self-serving, and works in the short term. Influence clarifies the truth, builds connection and trust, is audience-aware, and wins long-term loyalty. Influence is earned, not imposed. And good PR isn't about creating pressure; it's about creating resonance. Think about a brand you trust. Why do you trust it? Chances are, it's not because they yelled at you louder than anyone else. It's because their values match yours. Their story connects. Their voice feels consistent and clear. That's PR. That's influence.

"Publicists don't twist facts. We arrange them in a way that makes people care." (That's not spin, it's skill.) If that makes you uncomfortable, it might be because you've only experienced the bad side of PR. The empty hype. The vanity metrics. The loud, self-serving "look at me" energy. But real PR, the kind that shapes industries, moves hearts, and sparks dialogue, is grounded in truth, timing, and empathy.

PR Ain't About the Flash. It's About the Fit. Clients want flash, they want headlines, they want momentum yesterday. But flash fades. And if you're not ready when the spotlight hits, it'll burn you faster than it lit you up. That's why one of the most critical parts of the PR process is something most people skip: messaging development.

"Public Relations highlights your wins, places a band-aid over your losses, and buffs out any scratches that happen along the way." Let's break that down. Every publicist worth their retainer spends time:

- Understanding your internal landscape (brand, tone, values, goals)
- Exploring your public reputation (how people perceive you now)
- Evaluating your external environment (competitors, supporters, opponents)

That research becomes a strategy. That strategy becomes positioning. That positioning becomes the story. And if your story doesn't line up with the truth? We don't fake it; we fix it. But let's talk about the other reasons people might think PR is manipulation:

- They've hired the wrong person,
- Or they expected the wrong results.

Do you want to know when the "PR is a scam" comments typically appear? It's after someone pays $2,000 per month for two months and receives one quote in a mid-level blog. Or after a celebrity hires a high-powered firm but doesn't want to provide access, photos, or feedback. Or when someone pays $500 to a freelancer who guarantees them the cover of Forbes and delivers a Canva mockup instead. Here's the truth: PR takes time. PR takes participation. PR requires a proper budget, and PR is not the same as advertising.

PR does not guarantee coverage; most importantly, it works best when you work with it. Let's be real; some people don't like being "marketed to." They don't want to feel like someone crafted a message. They want it raw, real, "off the cuff." But here's the thing: raw doesn't mean real.

It just means unfiltered, and unfiltered doesn't always build trust. It often creates confusion, and that's where PR comes in. We don't write fiction. We take the truth and make it land. We craft the story for humans, not algorithms.

So, let's talk about the difference between spin and strategy using a real-world case, fictionalized but familiar.

Client A is facing a scandal: a leaked internal email reveals questionable comments made by an executive. The public expects a statement. Social is spiraling. Headlines are already circling.

Manipulation would say: "Let's blame it on a hack. Let's distract with a flashy campaign. Let's bury the email."

PR done right says: "We acknowledge what was said. We share how we're addressing it internally and externally. We commit to transparency as we advance."

One creates chaos; the other creates clarity. You don't need a smokescreen when you're willing to own the moment. That's what great PR does: it helps people own the moment in a way that aligns with values, responsibility, and the long game. We live in a culture where performance is currency. Where filters, followers, and "faking it 'til you make it" have become a business model. So, of course, when someone shows up looking polished, consistent, and intentional, people assume it must be fake.

Here's the twist: PR is not about being fake. It's about being intentional. And for many people, intentionality feels suspicious. However, the only thing more dangerous than a brand with no strategy is a brand pretending it doesn't need one.

If you've ever pitched yourself, your business, your book, or even your own value at a job interview, you've used PR. You've chosen what to say and what to leave out. You've highlighted your strengths and downplayed the messy parts. And that's not manipulation. That's communication. The key difference lies in how you approach it. Are you being truthful? Are you delivering value? Are you leading with clarity? Then it's not spin. It's the story. And a story, when done right, builds trust, culture, and connection.

As I mentioned or alluded to previously, we're living in the age of the PR stunt. Headline-hacking. Shock campaigns. Clickbait controversies. Some of it works because chaos is a compelling concept. But chaos without a follow-through plan is just noise. Real PR isn't just about grabbing attention. It's about keeping it. Let's look at two examples.

PR Stunt Gone Sideways:
A brand "accidentally" posts a controversial tweet. It goes viral. They release a vague apology. Sales spike, then tank the next quarter when customers realize there's no substance behind the stunt.

Strategic PR Done Right:
A brand launches a campaign addressing a social issue tied to its mission. They partner with trusted community leaders, center authentic voices, and use storytelling to educate. The buzz grows with integrity, and the loyalty lasts far beyond the campaign.

Guess which one built brand equity? PR's real power lies in shaping narratives, not disseminating fake news.

When used with intention, ethics, and empathy, PR has the power to change culture, shift conversations, elevate unheard voices, protect what matters, and build bridges in moments of breakdown.

That's not manipulation. That's leadership. Here's the deal. The people who yell "manipulation!" every time PR shows up are often the same people who:

- Don't show up prepared
- Don't know their message
- Don't understand timing
- Want results without input
- Expect overnight fame with no foundation

PR isn't the problem; the lack of strategy is. If this chapter has done anything, I hope it's helped you see PR isn't about faking a better story; it's about finding the story you already have and telling it in a way people will hear. We don't work in illusions. We work in insight. And the best PR? It doesn't trick people. It treats them like they matter.

Chapter Two – Debrief Notes

Reflection
Have you ever assumed a polished message was automatically dishonest? Why do you think that is? When have you personally experienced someone misunderstanding your intention because of how you presented your message?

What's your gut reaction to the word "spin"? Do you see a difference between spin and storytelling?

Reframe
What does "ethical influence" look like in your work or brand?
How can you intentionally shape your message without compromising your truth?

List three values your communication strategy should always reflect:

Action Challenge
Write a short brand statement (for yourself or a brand you work with) that aligns with truth, trust, and influence, not hype.

Example Format:
"We believe in [value], which is why we [action]. Our mission is to [result/impact]—with clarity, not chaos."
Your Turn:

Chapter Three

THE PUPPET MASTERS

"Publicists aren't pulling strings; we're cutting the ones keeping your message from moving while keeping the others from snapping."

   If PR people were truly puppet masters, wouldn't everything look a little more polished? Instead, most publicists are knee-deep in Google Docs at midnight, reworking messaging that changed at the last minute.
   They're calming a client who just did a podcast rant or ghostwriting a response to a tweet they begged that client not to post in the first place. We're not puppet masters. We're planners. We're translators. We're editors, educators, and emotional support strategists. We're the ones called when your ego has already hit "send."

I honestly believe Pop Culture and reality television made this myth feel real. From *Scandal to Ray Donovan to The West Wing*, PR is portrayed as the secret weapon behind the curtain. The person with the burner phone, the secret folder, and the "you didn't hear this from me" vibe. We've been cast as fixers. Sure, some of us have done our share of behind-the-scenes magic, but PR is often about preparation, not performance.

It's not control, it's coordination.

And trust me, if we were really controlling the story, half the mess you see online wouldn't make it past a group chat.

Much of the confusion surrounding PR stems from the disparity between what clients think we do and what we actually do.

- "Can you make me famous?"
- "I want to be on TV tomorrow."
- "I don't want to do interviews. Can you just handle it?"
- "I want press, but I don't want to talk about that thing everyone's asking me about."

Welcome to the wish list. A list of real quotes from real people who really thought that PR meant flipping a switch and becoming instantly influential.

Here's what we actually do:

What Clients Think	What PR Pros Do
Book press overnight	Research, develop, pitch, follow up, repeat
"Handle everything."	Create strategies with the client, not without
Guarantee results	Manage expectations and build long-term credibility
Make them sound perfect	Help them sound authentic, consistent and clear
Control the media	Cultivate relationships that earn trust and access

As I shared in Public Relations Ain't Free, scope is everything: "A publicist is not your manager, agent, assistant, or miracle worker. We're content strategists and brand builders who pitch your story to the right people, not every person."

Let's clarify the confusion:
- **Publicist**: Shapes your narrative, builds your media presence, and manages your public perception.
- **Manager**: Handles your long-term career moves, booking, negotiations, and strategic partnerships.
- **Agent**: Secures paid work and appearances.
- **Social Media Manager**: Manages online content, scheduling, and engagement.

If you expect one person to be all these roles, you're setting yourself (and your publicist) up for disappointment.

One of the primary reasons people believe in the "puppet master" myth is that they want to.

They want someone to take control. To make it easy. To make it fast. But PR doesn't work without partnership. And when clients expect complete control without collaboration, here's what happens:

- They don't provide timely responses
- They ghost during press follow-ups
- They change messaging mid-campaign
- They don't prepare for interviews
- They assume coverage equals conversion (it doesn't)

Then, when things don't go as planned? "PR doesn't work." Nah. What doesn't work is expecting a strategy to succeed without putting it into action.

I had a client early in my career who had a brand-new business and a beautiful brand. But no audience, credibility, or message beyond "Hire me, I'm great." We spent weeks developing angles, drafting a press release, and building a pitch list. We were ready to go. Then, the client went rogue, sent their own pitch to a major outlet, and got blocked.

They DM'd three journalists with generic "check out my business" messages. They ghosted their first interview opportunity because "they didn't feel like it." And then they said, "I thought you were supposed to be pulling the strings. Why isn't this working?" Because you're not a puppet, and I'm not here to make you dance. I'm here to help you connect. Strategically. Intentionally. Authentically.

Once again, pulling from the *What Does a Publicist Do chapter of Public Relations Ain't Free,* here's a real list of what publicists bring to the table:

Research
We thoroughly research your brand, industry, and audience before pitching any ideas.

Strategy
We develop a plan tailored to your goals, not a one-size-fits-all template.

Message Development
We help shape what you say and how you say it so people hear it.

Media List Building
We source relevant outlets, writers, producers, and editors.

Pitching
We pitch strategically and respectfully, not by spamming people.

Follow-Up & Coordination
We manage logistics, requests, interview prep, and press kits.

Monitoring & Reporting
We track placements and evaluate impact, not just clicks.
That's not control.
That's communication.
That's collaboration.

And it's *more than enough if* the client is actually ready.

Let's be honest: sometimes, clients do want to be in complete control. They don't want feedback. They don't want guardrails. They want a bullhorn, not a blueprint.

> They say, "I know my audience."
> They say, "I want to say it my way."
> They say, "People will get it."

But the media doesn't care about your intention. They care about your impact. One lousy interview can undo months of relationship-building. One off-brand statement can cost you a keynote. And when that happens, guess who gets blamed?

Yup, the publicist.

That being said, we're not here to control you. We're here to align you with your message, mission, and moment.
That means we will:

- Push back when the message is messy
- Recommend silence when the news cycle is loud
- Say "not yet" when a client wants to rush to press
- Advocate for clarity, not clout

Because while everyone else is reacting, we're responding. And that's what keeps brands from breaking.

As we close this chapter, highlighting that we're not puppet masters; we're message makers, let people think PR is just a trick. Let them believe we're behind the curtain, pulling strings. You and I know better. We're not creating illusions. We're creating alignment. And in an attention economy that rewards chaos, that's the most powerful thing a brand can have.

Chapter Three – Debrief Notes

Reflect
- Have you ever hired someone expecting them to "fix everything" without your full involvement?
- What are some expectations you've had around PR that may not align with how it actually works?
- Do you see the publicist as a teammate or a technician? Why?

Reframe
Publicists don't pull strings; they build strategy.
How can you better collaborate with a publicist (or communications partner) in your business or brand?

What are 2–3 areas of your messaging where you might expect results without doing your part?

Action Challenge
Set clear expectations for your next PR engagement (or self-led campaign):

Start Here:
"I understand that my publicist is responsible for, while I commit to showing up for."

Example:
"I understand that my publicist is responsible for shaping strategy and outreach, while I commit to showing up for interviews and preparing my message."

Now, it's your turn:

Chapter Four

CRISIS JUNKIES & SCANDAL WRANGLERS

"If you only call on PR when it's already on fire, don't be mad when we show up with a hose and not a miracle."

Public relations has a reputation problem, and it's never clearer than during a crisis. As soon as something goes wrong, you'll hear it:

"Must be the PR team behind that apology."
"Classic PR spin."
"They're just trying to save face."

And listen, they're not wrong. But they're also missing the point because crisis communication isn't about saving face; it's about saving trust.

It's about helping a brand or a person navigate a moment they may not survive alone and emerge with dignity, clarity, and accountability still intact.

It's not pretty.
It's not easy.
And it's not spin.

It's strategic, painful, high-stakes, surgical communication. PR doesn't create the crisis; it contains it. There's this Hollywood idea that PR people manufacture controversy just to "clean it up." Let me be clear: we don't need to create chaos. **It's already coming.**

No matter how polished one tweet, misquote, camera phone, or tone-deaf caption may be, every brand, leader, and entrepreneur is just a full-blown crisis away.

Our job isn't to hide that.
Our job is to manage the fallout, protect the credibility, and turn the moment into a message that restores some level of trust when possible.

And we don't do it with lies.
We do it with structure, speed, and strategy.

Let's break down what happens when PR gets the 9-1-1 call:

Assessment
- What happened?
- Who knows?
- Who is affected?
- What evidence is circulating?

Risk Management
- Is this a PR issue or a legal issue?
- What can we say publicly without creating liability?
- Messaging Framework
- What should be said now?
- What should not be said yet (or ever)?
- Who needs to speak and in what order?

Timing Strategy
- How fast is the news moving?
- What else is dominating the cycle?
- Is now the right time to speak, or is silence the strategy?

Tone + Delivery
- Is this an apology? A clarification? A redirect?
- Do we lead with empathy, authority, vulnerability, or urgency?

Follow-Up & Recovery
- Who needs a personal call?
- What will the next 30 days of messaging look like?
- How will we show growth, not just regret?

It's triage. It's therapy. It's leadership. And most of the time, we do it while everyone else is watching, waiting, and refreshing the feed.

What Most People Think Crisis PR Looks Like:

The Myth	The Reality
Writing the perfect apology	Guiding whether an apology is even needed
Fixing the media narrative	Containing the damage, not rewriting history
Keeping the truth hidden	Releasing the truth in a responsible way
Controlling public opinion	Rebuilding internal alignment first
Swooping in to "spin it pretty"	Slowing the spiral long enough to recover

"No 'spin' is strong enough to save you from poor leadership. There's only strategy, and you have to be willing to use it before you need it."
(Straight from the real trenches of PR)

Case Study:
The Brand That Waited Too Long

A client once waited **five days** to respond to a crisis.

The headlines were rolling.
Comment sections were flaming.
Screenshots were everywhere.

We begged them to respond gracefully, quickly, and clearly. But they didn't want to "give it more attention." They didn't want to "look guilty."
They wanted to "ride it out."

By the time we issued a statement, the audience had already formed their opinion.
The brand lost significant partnerships. Their team was demoralized.
And the apology, though honest, was too late.

Silence is not always a strategy; sometimes, it's a sign of surrender. You want the truth? It's not always the incident. It's the *response*.

Here's what takes a manageable crisis and turns it into a full-blown PR disaster:
- **Delays** in responding
- **Vague** or corporate-speak apologies
- **Defensiveness** from leadership
- **Blaming** or scapegoating
- **Deleting** content without a clear explanation
- **Doubling** down instead of owning it

The public doesn't expect perfection; they expect responsibility, and a good PR team will strive to maintain that responsibility as clearly, timely, and accurately as possible, even if it's uncomfortable.

Let's Talk "Cancel Culture"

You can't write a crisis chapter without talking about it. Is cancel culture real? Sure. But more often than not, what **people call "cancel culture" is actually accountability culture**.

And here's what we know in PR:
- You'll recover faster if your brand values are clear before the crisis.
- If your audience trusts you, they'll listen longer.
- Your apology won't feel like a cover-up if your messaging is consistent.

Being held accountable isn't the enemy. Being unprepared for it is. Crisis PR isn't just about public image but internal alignment. Before we ever issue a press statement, we ask:
- Do your employees know what's happening?
- Are your partners prepared for the blowback?
- Is your leadership aligned—or are you fractured behind the scenes?

Because the public can sense a disconnect, the worst thing you can do is issue a polished apology while your team is leaking screenshots from their inbox.

Fix *inside* before you post outside.

The reality of crisis work is that you can't always save the day, but you can save the future. Sometimes, the damage is done, the reputation is bruised, the trust is cracked, and no "statement" can fix everything. But that doesn't mean PR failed. That means reality showed up.

When that happens, here's what great PR does:
- It helps people own the truth, rather than hiding from it.
- It slows the chaos long enough for clarity to rise.
- It maps a path forward, not back.
- It reminds the world that imperfection isn't the end, inauthenticity is.

In closing, we're not here for the fireworks; we're here for the fallout. Don't call your PR team when it's already viral. Call us when something feels off. When you're about to post a caption that "might be too real." When your gut says, "Maybe not." Because PR isn't about handling chaos; it's about **avoiding unnecessary chaos** and navigating the rest gracefully.

We are not crisis junkies.
We are reputation architects.
And we don't just show up when it's broken.
We build it from the ground up.

Chapter Four Debrief Notes

When was the last time you experienced (or witnessed) a public or private crisis?

- What made the response effective or ineffective?
- Do you tend to address issues directly, or do you hope they blow over?
- How does your brand or business currently define "crisis"? (Think beyond just public backlash.)

Reframe

- What would it look like to approach crisis communication with clarity instead of panic?
- Think about your current messaging. Is it rooted in clear values that could withstand public scrutiny?

Write three values that should guide your brand in any crisis:

1. _____
2. _____
3. _____

Action Challenge

Create a Crisis Readiness Checklist for yourself or your team. Start here:

- I have a documented messaging framework for my brand
- I know who should speak on a public issue (e.g., spokesperson, CEO, etc.).
- I understand my legal limits and what can/can't be shared
- I've identified values that will anchor any public statement

- I can access approved assets (headshots, logos, press contacts) within 30 minutes
- My team is aligned on how we respond when the unexpected happens

How many boxes can you honestly check today?

Chapter Five

THE STRATEGY SYNDICATE

"Everyone wants to be seen. PR makes sure it's for the right reasons, in the right places, by the right people."

Let's start here: PR is not performance; PR is **positioning**. It's the work you do before the spotlight hits. It's why a pitch lands, a message resonates, or a brand suddenly becomes "everywhere" all at once. And the truth is, most people who complain that "PR doesn't work" never actually invested in a strategy; they invested in visibility.

They invested in attention. They skipped the foundation and wondered why the house fell down when the winds of public opinion hit. Here's the thing: visibility without clarity is a waste. You can be seen all day long and still not be understood, and that misunderstanding is what kills trust, momentum, and long-term value. So, what do we mean by "strategy" in PR? Let's break it down.

The Four Core Pillars of Real PR Strategy Research

"If you don't know the story behind the story, you're just throwing spaghetti at a media wall."

Good PR starts with understanding three things:
- Your internal landscape (your goals, values, history, offers, audience)
- Your current public perception (what people already think or say)
- Your external environment (competition, industry noise, cultural climate)

Your SWOT (Strengths, Weaknesses, Opportunities, Threats) analysis lives here. It's not sexy, but it's necessary because your story doesn't exist in a vacuum.

Positioning

"You can't pitch what you haven't positioned." Positioning is about defining who you are and, more importantly, who you're *not*. It includes:
- What makes you relevant
- Why your message matters right now
- Where do you fit into the bigger conversation
- How your tone and language make your message distinct

It's not about creating a persona; it's about aligning your story with truth, timing, and the needs of your audience.

Message Development
"The clearer your message, the less you have to explain it;" this is where the real magic happens. You've got your research. You've clarified your position. Now, it's time to **write it down, shape it, and pressure test it**. A solid messaging framework includes:
- Core brand story
- Media-friendly bio
- 3–5 key messages that you *repeat everywhere*
- Sample interview answers
- Reactive statements (for moments when you're under fire)
- Approved language (words you always use and words you never will)

This is the difference between "What do I say?" and "I'm ready."

Pitch Strategy & Execution
"Pitching is not praying. It's pattern-matching." Now, and only now, do we pitch. That means:
- Identifying the right media outlets
- Matching your angle to their audience and editorial tone
- Customizing each pitch (no spray-and-pray)
- Following up without being annoying
- Tracking coverage and building relationships for the long term

Every pitch isn't about promotion. Sometimes, it's about position. It's about planting the seed that says, 'This person belongs in the room.'

"If you're not ready to share your message clearly, you're not ready for PR. Hype will get you noticed, strategy will get you remembered." (Public Relations Ain't Free)

One of the biggest mistakes people make is hiring a publicist before they know what they want to be known for. PR doesn't create the product. It doesn't invent the purpose. It doesn't replace your voice. It *amplifies* what's already there. So, if what's there is messy, scattered, inconsistent, or unclear, that's exactly what people will see, just on a larger scale; this is how "strategy is optional" clients tend to emerge. You've seen them.

- They say, "I just want press."
- They don't want to go through messaging workshops.
- They ghost when you ask for bios or headshots.
- They reject your pitches because "it doesn't feel viral enough."
- They want visibility, but they haven't clarified their value.

Those clients? They're not building a brand. They're chasing clout, and PR is not a clout strategy; it's a *connection* strategy.

Case Study:
When Strategy Changed the Story

One client came in with a big personality, a new book, and a ton of buzz. But the message? All over the place. She was saying different things in every interview. Her website didn't match her IG bio. Her one sheet had outdated stats. Every outlet we pitched had a different version of who she was. We hit pause, went back to square one, and rebuilt her positioning from the inside out. Once we aligned the message across every touchpoint, everything shifted. Coverage increased, followers stayed (not just clicked), and podcast hosts invited her back. That's the power of clarity.

Everyone loves a viral moment. A trending soundbite. A screenshot of the "as seen in" logo. But you know what gets you invited back? What makes people quote you in boardrooms and classrooms? What earns trust in crowded, skeptical, scroll-happy markets? **Strategy**. And PR strategy isn't something you skip; it's something you sharpen because the goal isn't just to be known; the goal is to be known **for something that sticks**.

Chapter Five – Debrief Notes

Reflect
- Have you ever launched something before you had a clear message or strategy? How did it go?
- What's one way you've relied on visibility instead of clarity in your business or brand?
- When you think of "positioning," do you think about competitors or your own message?

Reframe
- What is the core message you want to be known for?
- What's one place where your messaging might be unclear or inconsistent?

Write three statements you want to anchor your brand story around:

1. _____
2. _____
3. _____

Action Challenge
Complete this sentence to clarify your current PR strategy (or where you want to go):

"I want to be known for _____, by _____, in places like _____."

Now, reverse-engineer your messaging to make that possible. Ask yourself:
- Do my media bios reflect this?
- Are my social profiles aligned with this positioning?
- Is my pitch matching the rooms I want to be in?

Chapter Six

THE RELATIONSHIP HUSTLE

"Public relations isn't about who you know; it's about how you show up for them repeatedly."

Let's make this plain: PR is not just a visibility business. It's a relationship business, and if you're not building genuine, consistent, and respectful connections with your audience and the media, then you're not doing PR effectively. You're promoting without relationships, like shouting into a hurricane, loud but powerless.

One of the most damaging ideas about PR is that publicists simply call their media friends and get you placed; that's like saying chefs just call their ingredients,

and the dish cooks itself. No. A media relationship is a carefully built, earned dynamic. It's:
- Trust
- Value
- Timing
- Respect
- Relevance

You don't just know a journalist. You serve them. You help them. You understand their beat, deadlines, audience, and style, and when your pitch lands in their inbox, they don't say, "Oh, it's my friend!" They say, "This is useful; this is good. I know this publicist doesn't waste my time." "Media relationships aren't automatic; they're built like every other relationship: with time, consistency, and mutual benefit." (Public Relations Ain't Free)

When you work with a publicist who respects the hustle of relationship-building, you're not just buying their email list but investing in their credibility. And that credibility can't be manufactured. It's grown through:
- Quality pitches
- Honesty when a story isn't right
- Follow through on requests
- Not over-promising
- Not name-dropping when it doesn't apply

Media professionals are overworked, underpaid, flooded with 300+ pitches daily, working on five deadlines at once, and being told to chase traffic instead of truth. So if your pitch is generic, off-topic, too self-promotional, or clearly mass-sent, you're not just wasting your time; you're burning trust, and once you're on the "nah" list? It's a long road back.

The relationship hustle doesn't stop with the media. As a brand, a founder, or a thought leader, your relationships with:
- Your audience
- Your partners
- Your team
- Your collaborators
- Your community

... is *your PR pipeline*.

Every post you share, every caption you write, every podcast you're on, and every email you send shapes how people feel about you, and that's PR in its purest form: the emotional residue of your message.

Case Study:
The One Pitch That Changed Everything

Years ago, I had a client with a niche business and zero name recognition. We crafted her messaging, identified key outlets, and sent a targeted pitch to one journalist who might be interested; the pitch was personalized, sharp, and useful. That journalist passed but introduced me to someone else who ran the story, which went viral in her industry. That visibility led to a national feature. That feature led to speaking engagements, product sales, and licensing deals. All from one *respectful pitch*. Not from a connection or a favor but from a *relationship built in real-time* with care.

The Follow-Up Formula

Following up is an art form. Too little, and your pitch gets buried. Too much, and you get blocklisted. Here's the formula:

- Follow up after 3–5 business days.
- Reference the original pitch briefly.
- Provide one new update or hook (if available).
- Be respectful. Always offer an easy "no."

Example:

I wanted to follow up on my pitch from earlier this week regarding [Subject]. I know you're flooded, so there's no pressure; I just wanted to flag that [timely update/visual/angle]. Please let me know if this might be a good fit or if it's not the right time. Appreciate your work either way!

Easy. Clean. Human.

What Happens When You Play the Long Game
People think relationships are soft skills. Intangible. Optional. But here's what a well-managed PR relationship can earn you:
- Multiple placements from the same outlet over time
- Last-minute inclusion in roundups or trend stories
- Exclusive opportunities before they're public
- Invitations to speak, comment, or collaborate
- *Trust*, even when the story is difficult

That's not luck; that's labor, that's PR.

Final word: show up when you don't need anything.

Want to Build Better PR Relationships?

- Share the story without being featured.
- Support the journalist without pitching.
- Say "thank you" without asking for more.
- Be a source of value, not just a source.

Your pitch gets opened when your reputation is built on respect, service, and substance, not because they owe you but because they know you.

Chapter Six – Debrief Notes

Reflect
- When was the last time you built a relationship with someone in media, not to get something, but to offer value?
- What kind of experiences have you had with pitching—either giving or receiving? What worked? What didn't?
- Have you ever made the mistake of focusing on attention over connection?

Reframe
- Relationships are the engine of public relations. Where could you cultivate stronger media, audience, or partner relationships in your business or brand?

Write three people, platforms, or communities where you want to deepen your connection:

1. _____
2. _____
3. _____

Action Challenge
Craft a simple relationship-building outreach email to a journalist, podcaster, or partner you admire without asking for anything.

"Hey [Name], I just wanted to say I appreciate your work on [specific story/topic]. Your approach to [value/topic] really stands out. I'll be sharing it with my community—it's exactly the kind of insight people need right now. Grateful for what you do."

Set a goal to send at least one of these messages each week for the next month.

Chapter Seven

THE BRAND WHISPERERS

"Brand isn't just what people say about you; it's what they remember when you're not talking."

Branding is often mistaken for logos and color palettes, but branding is deeper, stickier, and quieter. It's the way people feel when your name comes up in a meeting.

It's the story people tell about you after they've scrolled past your post. It's the energy, the essence, the consistency that lingers long after the spotlight moves. And publicists? We're not just storytellers. We're **brand whisperers**. We help your audience understand *who you are* before you've even said a word.

Ask someone what their brand is, and they'll say things like, "I help people scale their business," "I'm a

motivational speaker," "I'm a clean beauty brand," or "I'm a wellness coach for women of color." Cool. But if I strip the buzzwords, what's left? Because here's the truth:
- If your story could be copied and pasted onto someone else's website? It's not a brand.
- Does your tone change across different platforms? It's not a brand.
- If your audience can't describe you in one sentence? It's not a brand, it's a *broadcast*.

Publicists aren't here to give you a new identity; we're here to find the thread inside what you're already doing and pull it until it forms a straightforward, unforgettable narrative. We help you:
- Clarify your message
- Define your voice
- Align your values with your visuals
- Translate who you are into something *relatable, repeatable, and respected*

That's not magic, that's method, and it's what makes a brand last longer than a launch.

"If your brand is confusing, no one's going to sit around and decode it. People don't chase clarity. They respond to it."
(Public Relations Ain't Free)

One of the most significant problems I see is that people want to be in the press but don't know what they want to be known for.

Before you pitch a story, a product, or a platform, ask:
- What impression do I want to leave?
- What's the experience of my brand?

- If I walked away right now, what would people say?

If the answer isn't consistent, your message won't land because consistency *is* clarity.

The Three Layers of Brand Identity (That PR Touches Every Day)

Voice
- Is it casual, bold, warm, professional, poetic, or direct?
- Is it yours, or are you mimicking someone else's?

Values
- What do you stand for?
- What won't you do no matter the offer?

Vibe
- How do you make people *feel*?
- Is your tone aligned across platforms?

Once these layers are clear, every pitch, post, podcast, and partnership becomes easier to navigate because now, you're not guessing; you're building from the center.

Case Study:
The Brand That Looked the Part
But Didn't Say Anything

A client once came to me with *beautiful* branding.
The website? Flawless.

The packaging? Luxe.
The social media? Consistent, aesthetically.

But when I asked, "What's the story?" they paused. They couldn't explain what made them different. They didn't have a founder story or content that educated or empowered their audience. Everything looked perfect, but it felt hollow.
We began by finding their voice, shaping the founder's 'why,' building brand pillars to ground their messaging, and crafting three key story angles for PR outreach. Within months, the difference was night and day.

Customers connected, the media responded, and the *brand* finally had a heartbeat.

Don't get it twisted: there's a difference between **branding** and **personal branding**. Branding is the perception of a company, product, or movement, while personal branding is how you show up as a leader or voice, but the rules are the same:
- You need a clear story
- You need to stand for something
- You need to be consistent across platforms
- You need to sound like yourself everywhere

Publicists help align those elements so you're not one person in an interview and another on Instagram Live, because when your presence is fragmented, your influence is too.

The Brand Whisperer's Real Power: Shaping What Lasts

Flashy launches fade, and one viral hit does not a legacy make, but when your brand is rooted in clarity, consistency, and connection? You build community, you build trust, and you build staying power. That's why PR pros aren't just out here chasing clips; we're building frameworks. Frameworks that:

- Tell the right story
- To the right audience
- At the right moment
- With the right energy

Over. And over. And over again.

Chapter Seven – Debrief Notes

Reflect
- How would someone describe your brand after interacting with it for just 10 seconds?
- Are you consistently presenting yourself with the same voice, tone, and intention across all platforms?
- Where have you seen branding done really well, and what made it memorable?

Reframe
- What values drive your voice?
- What *feelings* do you want your audience to associate with you?

Write a "brand clarity mantra" below:

"I help _____ feel _____ through _____."

Now try to write your brand's one-liner—no fluff:

"We're the brand that _____."

Action Challenge
Audit your own public presence:
- My bio clearly reflects my values and work
- My tone is consistent across IG, LinkedIn, email, and my website
- My audience could describe what I do without me prompting them
- My brand feels aligned with my actual energy, not what I think will sell

If you can't check three or more, it's time to refine your brand voice with intention.

Chapter Eight

THE DIGITAL DETECTIVES

"The internet never forgets, but PR can help shape what it remembers."

There was a time when PR consisted mainly of press releases, newspaper clippings, and TV segments. Now? It's also comment sections, DMs, podcast quotes, podcast reactions, reposted tweets, deep-dive TikToks, Google results, and screen-recorded stories that you *thought* disappeared.

Today's publicist is part storyteller, part strategist, and **part digital detective** because perception lives online now, and if you're not paying attention to your digital footprint, someone else is.

Somewhere along the lines, people began to believe online reputations only affected influencers; nope! If your name, brand, or business is searchable, **you have a reputation**, and that reputation is shaped by:
- What you post
- What others post about you
- What's left unsaid
- What's outdated
- And what could be found with a quick scroll or Google search

So, yes, public relations today means digital relations, which means knowing how to monitor, manage, and adapt to the speed of the internet. Here's what modern PR pros are doing (quietly and constantly):
- Monitoring brand mentions and keywords
- Tracking SEO search trends around a person or product
- Auditing Google results for outdated/inaccurate content
- Managing Wikipedia edits (if applicable)
- Helping clean up the online presence for potential media or partnerships
- Responding to misinformation quickly and strategically
- Advising on platform-specific tone and voice for consistency
- Identifying opportunities to elevate brand authority, not just visibility

This isn't fluff; this is digital reputation insurance. PR and SEO used to be two different teams. Now? They're married. Effective PR helps you rank online without needing to pay for ads. How?

- Media placements on high-authority sites link back to your website
- Well-written bylines and guest posts boost your brand authority
- Interviews help you own your story on searchable platforms
- Consistent mentions across the web reinforce your credibility with algorithms

Think of it this way:
- PR = visibility + trust
- SEO = findability + relevance
- Put them together, and your brand becomes *discoverable AND believable.*

Let's say someone Googles you or your business and they find:
- A Facebook page you haven't updated since 2017
- A low-res headshot
- An article from four years ago that doesn't match your current direction
- A broken website link
- No current features, mentions, or media

You might be excellent, but the internet doesn't know that, and unfortunately, neither does your potential client, investor, producer, or reader; this is where digital PR shows up:

Updating bios

- Reclaiming outdated narratives
- Optimizing your "About" page
- Curating interviews or placements that reflect your *now*

Case Study:
The Thought Leader Who Was MIA Online

A high-powered client came to us, ready to speak on national stages. She had the experience, credentials, story – everything except a visible footprint.

Her website wasn't mobile-friendly, she didn't have high-quality media headshots, her last interview was four years old, there were no consistent backlinks, no one had tagged her in a recent story, and Google showed someone else with the same name ranking higher.

So we built:
- A fresh digital press kit
- Two bylined articles on major sites
- A podcast tour focused on SEO-friendly keywords
- Consistent media mentions in her niche

Six months later? She was the first and only result that mattered, and she finally looked online like she had already shown up in person.

Modern PR isn't just about what you're saying; it's about what's being said about you. So we listen:
- We scan forums, comment sections, and Reddit threads
- We use tools to track sentiment and keywords
- We identify rising conversations and prep you to speak into them
- We see where your audience lives, and how *they talk*

Because if you're not listening, your message won't land. You'll be shouting into a room that has already left.

As we go through this chapter. Let's be clear about what Digital PR isn't.
- It's not paying for fake followers
- It's not keyword stuffing or backlink buying
- It's not deleting every criticism
- It's not AI-written press with no human context

Digital PR is human-first; it's built on:
- Authority
- Authenticity
- Alignment

It's how you show up when people are already searching.

Final Word: Own the Search. Shape the Story.
If you want to be credible in this age, you can't just be present; you need to be *positioned*, because someone will Google you.

The question is: will what they find match what you say? Modern PR ensures the answer is yes, not by creating illusions but by creating alignment between your voice, values, and visibility **across every digital touchpoint.**

Chapter Eight – Debrief Notes

Reflect
- What comes up when you Google yourself, your brand, or your business?
- Does it align with who you are now?
- Have you ever been overlooked for an opportunity that a stronger digital presence could've helped?

Reframe
- What part of your online presence needs the most attention?

    ☐ Bio ☐ SEO ☐ Media mentions

    ☐ Google results ☐ Social tone

- What do you want people to feel or understand about you from your digital footprint?

Write your digital presence goal in one sentence:

"I want to show up online as _____."

Action Challenge
Choose **two** of the following to complete this week:
- Update your "About" page with your current focus and values
- Google yourself in an incognito window, note what shows up on page one
- Choose a high-traffic platform (LinkedIn, IG, Medium) and revise your bio
- Create or update your press kit with a headshot, one-liner, and contact info

Identify one publication or podcast that aligns with your brand, and pitch yourself

Chapter Nine

THE ANTI-PR PR MOVEMENT

"Don't say you don't believe in PR while building your entire brand on PR strategy."

There's a trend happening; have you noticed it? Influencers, CEOs, founders, and even thought leaders proudly say: "We don't do PR," "We built our brand without any public relations help," and "I don't need press. My audience is my PR."

But let's zoom out; they're telling stories, shaping public perception, crafting messaging, and leading movements. That is PR; they just don't want to admit they're doing it. This chapter is for the entrepreneurs who say:
- "My brand grew organically."

- "I just speak from the heart, I don't have a strategy."
- "We don't do polished messaging. We're real."

You do have a strategy; you just don't call it that. You're using:
- Positioning
- Brand voice
- Story arcs
- Visual consistency
- Community engagement
- Press-worthy social proof

You are using PR, and you've just disconnected it from its name. Here's the irony: the people saying "we don't do PR" are often exceptional at it. They:
- Curate their image
- Respond to controversy on-brand
- Time their launches for peak engagement
- Partner with platforms that expand their reach
- Align their language with the audience's emotions

That's public relations. That's strategy. That's the whole game.

> "PR is often invisible until it's done wrong. That's why people think they don't need it. When it works, they forget it was ever at play." (Public Relations Ain't Free)

Just because your PR didn't include a traditional agency or publicist doesn't mean it didn't exist.

You were still:
- Building your reputation
- Shaping perception
- Navigating narratives
- Managing digital presence

PR without a publicist is possible, but PR without intention? That's dangerous.

Case Study:
The Brand That "Didn't Need PR"
(Until They Did)

A founder had built a strong, loud, community-led business with no formal publicists or press releases; everything was grassroots: DMs, Reels, podcasts, and word of mouth. Then came the controversy; a comment went viral for the wrong reasons, and they were suddenly on the defensive. There was no press statement, prepared spokesperson, clearly published brand values, or media ally to help reframe the narrative. Their "no PR needed" vibe quickly became "Where's the PR team?" Even if you don't engage with the press, if you don't run traditional campaigns, or even if you never hire a publicist, you're still in the PR game. Every comment, post, caption, email, podcast, and screenshot contributes to shaping your brand. You don't get to opt out; you only get to choose whether you're doing it *intentionally*.

What "We Don't Do PR" Usually Means

Let's decode it:

What They Say	What They Usually Mean
"We don't do PR."	We don't hire agencies, but we manage our image.
"Our growth was organic."	We leveraged word-of-mouth + curated content.
"We don't chase press."	We've built brand equity, and the media now come to us.
"We're real, not polished."	We use storytelling that feels unfiltered.

Let's stop acting like "not doing PR" is noble; it's just a different approach, and guess what? Both approaches require intention, consistency, and a strategic approach.

You don't have to lie.
You don't have to polish everything.
You don't have to "be corporate."

But you need to be understood if you're building a business, movement, or mission. You need people to trust you, follow you, support you, and believe in your voice, and that doesn't happen by accident; it happens through public relations.

Done well.
Done with *integrity*.
Done *on purpose.*

Chapter Nine – Debrief Notes

Reflect
- Have you ever avoided PR because it felt too "corporate" or inauthentic?
- Have you benefited from PR (visibility, messaging, perception) without realizing it?

Reframe
- What would embracing PR as a clarity and connection tool look like instead of just visibility?
- How can you talk about your strategy openly without distancing yourself from the language of PR?

Write a truth about your current approach:
"I've been practicing PR by _____, even if I didn't call it that."

Action Challenge
1. Pick one "organic" thing you're already doing (e.g., podcasting, brand storytelling, collaborations).
2. Map out a short PR plan around it.

Ask:
- What's the message?
- Who does this serve?
- Where could this visibility go next (press, podcast, panel, etc.)?

Use what you're already doing, but do it on purpose now.

Chapter Ten

WHEN PR FAILS

"Bad PR doesn't mean PR is bad. It means it wasn't aligned, strategic, or honest."

Let's be honest with ourselves and each other: **PR doesn't always work**. Sometimes, it fails because it wasn't the right time; sometimes, it fails because the wrong person was hired; and sometimes, it fails because the brand wasn't ready.

The worst thing about PR gone wrong isn't the money lost; it's the trust lost; that's why this chapter exists, not to scare you off PR, but to show you what happens when the process is misused, rushed, or misunderstood.

One of the most dangerous narratives about PR right now is, "I paid for PR and got nothing. So it must be a scam." But let's unpack that. Did you:

- Have a clear message and strategy?
- Timely provide your publicist with access and assets?
- Stick to your tone and trust their timeline?
- Expect press without positioning?

If the answer is "no," you didn't get scammed, you got started too early, or you didn't have a solid foundation.

"Public Relations Ain't Free, but it also ain't magic." *(Truth from the trenches.)*

Common Reasons PR Doesn't Deliver

- **No Strategy**
  - There is no brand story, unclear messaging, and no angles to pitch.

- **Poor Fit**
  - The publicist didn't understand your niche, tone, or goals.

- **Lack of Participation**
  - The client ghosted the process, missed interviews, and delayed responses.

- **Unrealistic Expectations**
  - Wanting viral press with no assets or audience foundation.

- **Bad Timing**
  - Launches with no newsworthy hook, pitching during major global crises.

- **Overpromising PR Providers**
    - Anyone who guarantees media placements (without disclaimers)?

There's a new crop of "PR experts" who sell press like it's a vending machine:
- "Get featured in Forbes for $297!"
- "We'll put you in 10 publications in 10 days!"
- "Instant media exposure guaranteed!"

These are often:
- Low-quality, pay-to-play platforms
- Non-editorial features that look like press but hold no journalistic weight
- One-time mentions that don't build long-term credibility

They're not illegal, but they're also not public relations. Real PR is earned, not bought, and it's about *building relationships*, *not just collecting* receipts.

So, how do you know you're ready? Ask yourself:
- Do I know what story I'm telling and why now?
- Have I clearly defined my audience and value?
- Do I have visuals, bios, and assets ready?
- Am I willing to partner with my publicist, not just pay them?
- Am I prepared for consistent momentum, not just one viral moment?

If the answer is yes? You're ready. If not? You're better off waiting. PR isn't a band-aid. It's a blueprint.

So, what do you do when PR doesn't work? Let's say you did everything right and still didn't get the traction you hoped for. Here's what to do next:

- **Review the Metrics**
  - *What did happen?* Traffic? Social engagement? Reputation shift?

- **Refine the Message**
  - Were people confused? Uninterested? Did the story miss the moment?

- **Rebuild with a New Timeline**
  - Sometimes, the story needs to evolve, or you may pitch too soon.

- **Ask for an Honest Debrief**
  - A real PR pro will tell you what worked and what didn't.

Don't Ghost the Process

PR builds over time. One short campaign isn't the whole game. If PR feels like it failed you, don't just walk away bitter; look deeper. Was it:

- The strategy?
- The messaging?
- The timeline?
- The expectations?
- The execution?

Because when all five of those align? PR works. Period.

Case Study: When PR Was the Right Tool at the Wrong Time

A startup founder sought national coverage immediately after launch, despite having no product reviews, customers, or testimonials, only a compelling concept and an Instagram page.

We explained: "Let's spend 90 days building your positioning and brand identity." They said no, hired someone else who promised press *immediately*, and the result? One feature on a niche blog. $6,000 spent. No traffic. No sales.

Six months later, they came back. We rebuilt their foundation, and three strong placements followed. This time, they were ready. PR wasn't the problem; **timing and trust** were.

Chapter Ten – Debrief Notes

Reflect
- Have you ever felt disappointed by a visibility or PR experience? What part of that experience still sticks with you?
- Do you tend to expect instant results, or are you prepared for the long game?
- Have you ever hired someone to fix a branding or PR problem that was actually a deeper business issue?

Reframe
- Instead of "Did PR work for me?" ask:
- "Was I truly ready for public visibility—and did I invest in the right strategy?"
- Write your PR readiness statement:
- "I will feel confident investing in PR when _____."

Action Challenge

Take inventory of your current PR assets:
- Brand bio
- Visual identity
- Website or landing page
- Founder or brand story
- Media kit
- Previous coverage or testimonials

If any of these are missing or outdated, set a timeline to refresh and align them before your next media push.

Chapter Eleven

THE COMEBACK CODE

"Your reputation doesn't end with a scandal. It ends when you stop showing up with a strategy."

Redemption is real, but it doesn't happen by accident, and in the world of public relations, comebacks are built, not given. We've seen it over and over again:
- The celebrity who made a mistake, then made a thoughtful return.
- The founder, who weathered backlash, then rebuilt their brand stronger.
- The brand that went silent came back with transparency, service, and impact.

Behind every powerful comeback? A **communications plan**.

People believe reputations are like tattoos; once you're marked, it's permanent, but that's not how PR works. That's not how humans work. People mess up, brands evolve, and movements stumble, but when you lead with **accountability, consistency**, and clarity, the public doesn't just forgive; they respect the effort.

Because what people are really looking for isn't perfection; it's the growth they can see, so when the story shifts, so should the strategy. Every brand or person who's been through a public misstep needs to do three things:

1. **Own it**
   - Be honest. Be clear. Be early.
   - Denial fuels drama. Ownership defuses it.

2. **Align actions with words.**
   - What you say publicly must match what you do privately.
   - Trust isn't restored with talk; it's rebuilt with movement.

3. **Show up over time.**
   - One good statement won't erase months of controversy.
   - Stay consistent. Let people see the change, not just hear it.

This is where PR thrives, at the intersection of growth and visibility.

Case Study: The Comeback No One Saw Coming

A CEO was caught on camera making a wildly inappropriate joke, which went viral. Sponsors pulled out, partners paused, and everyone assumed they were done, but behind the scenes:

- A PR team was already in place.
- A full apology was issued within 24 hours with no excuses.
- The CEO stepped back and stepped up, donating to relevant causes, attending listening sessions, and restructuring their team.
- Press outreach was paused for 90 days.

The next time the brand appeared? It was with new leadership, community partnerships, and a clear message: "We changed because we had to. Now we're showing you how."

Did everyone forgive? No. But the brand survived, and eventually, it thrived again. You can't manipulate your way back into trust, you can't silence dissent and expect applause, and you can't disappear and expect relevance to wait for you.

What you *can* do is:
- Apologize without deflecting
- Acknowledge harm without centering your own pain
- Ask what's needed and respond with service
- Show up again and again with humility and clarity

Because real PR doesn't just protect reputation; it rebuilds relationships. The truth? Most people don't remember what you did wrong; they remember how you handled it. Were you cold? Defensive? Evasive? Or were you real? Present? Accountable?

The long game isn't just about restoring your image; it's about earning a new kind of respect. Some of the most iconic brands, leaders, and businesses didn't reach legendary status because they never made mistakes; they reached it because they handled challenging moments well.

Final Word: Your Reputation Is Not a Sentence. It's a Series.
You get to write the next chapter, but don't just wing it; *plan* it. Work with your PR team, gather your community, check your ego at the door, and rebuild as if your integrity depends on it, because it does.

Chapter Eleven – Debrief Notes

Reflect
- Have you ever witnessed a comeback you respected? What made it powerful or believable?
- Did you hide, defend, or respond when you've made mistakes in your brand or business?

Reframe
- If something were to happen today, would you know how to react?
- What would it take to own your story—even the messy parts?

Write your redemption-ready mindset below:

"If I fall, I will lead with _____."

Action Challenge
Draft your **reputation repair checklist:**
- I know who should speak on behalf of my brand.
- I have key brand values that guide my public responses.
- I have a plan for pausing, not disappearing, in the event of a crisis.
- I know how to work with a publicist to rebuild intentionally.
- I'm clear on what accountability looks like for me and my brand.

Chapter Twelve

THE FINALE

Well! Look at that; this isn't the end; it's a new starting point. This book wasn't about teaching you how to "get famous." It was about teaching you how to get **intentional** because public relations isn't about perfection; it's about **positioning**, **purpose**, and **people**. It's about using your voice on purpose, telling your story on your terms, and showing up when things are good and real.

You don't need to become someone else to earn press; you don't need to chase attention to gain authority; you just need clarity, consistency, and the courage to stop hiding behind "not being ready."

Here's the truth: **you are already someone's story worth telling**. But if you don't tell it, someone else will. So this is your invitation:

To get visible.
To get strategic.
To speak louder, not because you want noise, but because you have something to say.

Public Relations Ain't Free, not in effort, energy, or truth. But when done well? It's one of the most powerful tools you'll ever have.

Use it wisely.
Use it honestly.
Use it now.

Thank you for reading!

The Great PR Heist: How Public Perception Stole the Truth about PR

Resources

You've made it through the myth-busting, curtain-pulling, perception-shifting truth about PR, and now it's time to put it into action.

The following pages are packed with free tools, templates, and strategic prompts designed to help you apply what you've learned.

From media pitch scripts to visibility checklists and budget breakdowns, these resources were created to meet you where you are and move you forward.

Whether you're launching your first campaign or elevating your existing brand, this toolkit is your bridge from insight to execution. Let's go.

Essential PR Assets Checklist

Before you pitch, post, or go public, make sure these are in place:

- Branded Bio (Short + Long)
- Press-Ready Headshots
- One-Sheet or Media Kit
- Talking Points
- Key Brand Messages (3–5 core truths you want repeated)
- Company Overview or About Page
- Website or Digital Home Base
- Recent Coverage or Testimonials (if available)
- Social Media Profiles (Updated + Aligned)
- Clear CTA: How should people contact or book you?

Media Pitch Template (Cold Email Format)

Subject Line Ideas:
- Story Idea: [Topic] That's Resonating with [Audience]
- Thought Leader in [Industry] Changing the Conversation on [Topic]
- Timely Story Angle: [Your Name] on [Issue]

Pitch Body:
Hi [Journalist's Name],

I'm reaching out with a story idea that may be a strong fit for your audience at [Outlet Name]. My client, [Your Name], is a [Your Title or Description] with a unique perspective on [Topic].

In short:
- [1–2 sentence hook: What makes this timely or relevant?]
- [Brief summary of your work or insight: Why you?]
- [Include a website or media kit link if available.]

We'd be honored to support any coverage you're developing around [related topic or theme]. If this isn't a fit right now, I appreciate your time either way!

Warmly,

[Your Name]

[Contact Info]

[Link to Website or IG]

Thought Leader Bio Builder

[Full Name] is a [Title/Profession] known for [Core Strength or Unique Offering]. As the [Founder/Creator] of [Company or Brand], [He/She/They] helps [Audience] [Achieve Desired Outcome] through [Methodology or Signature Approach].

With [# of Years] in [Industry], [Your Name] has been featured in [Notable Placements, if any] and spoken at [Event/Institution] on [Topic or Expertise]. Passionate about [Belief or Value], [He/She/They] continues to champion [Cause] through work that's rooted in [Key Themes].

Five Must-Know PR Terms

Term	What It Means
Media Pitch	A brief email or message offering a story idea to a journalist or outlet
Press Kit	A branded folder with your bio, photos, company info, and contact details
Embargo	A request that the media not publish a story before a specific date/time
Byline	An article you write that's published under your name in a media outlet
Earned Media	Publicity gained through story value, not paid placements or ads

Starter Media List

For Lifestyle & Culture Stories:
- Essence
- Refinery29
- Blavity
- xoNecole

- Popsugar

For Thought Leadership & Business:
- Forbes (Women / Entrepreneurs / Next 1000)
- Business Insider
- Fast Company
- Inc.
- The Grio

For Podcasts:
- The Brown CEO
- Side Hustle Pro
- She Did That
- Earn Your Leisure
- The Dream (depending on your theme)

Bonus Toolkit: The Media Mindset Worksheet
Get your mind right before pitching, posting, or "PRing" yourself.

What's Your Media Identity?
Complete these prompts to clarify how you want to be seen:
1. **I want to be known as someone who:**
   - _____

2. **The three topics I want to lead conversations around are:**
   - _____
   - _____
   - _____

3. **If someone Googled me today, the first impression I'd want them to have is:**
   - _____

Message Clarity Check-In
Ask yourself before any pitch, podcast, post, or partnership:
- Is this message **true to my voice?**
- Is it **aligned with my values?**
- Does it serve a **clear audience or intention?**
- Am I saying something new, or just saying something?

If it doesn't pass all four, pause and reshape.

Pitch Prep Checklist (Quick Fire)
Before you hit, send:
- Does the subject line match the value of the pitch?
- Did I tailor this to the journalist's outlet and audience?
- Can I summarize the story in 2 punchy sentences?
- Do I have a credible, well-written bio or link ready?
- Is there a hook tied to something timely, cultural, or unique?

Bonus: Always ask, *Why should anyone care about this right now?*

Power Pitch Angle Prompts
If you're stuck, try starting here:
"What no one's talking about in [your industry] and why it matters now."

"The thing most people get wrong about [your expertise] and how to fix it."

"Why [popular trend] is backfiring and what to do instead."

"The surprising connection between [cultural moment] and [your field]."

"Behind the scenes of the PR strategy that saved a brand's reputation."

PR Budget Planning Worksheet
Because exposure without intention is just expensive noise.

Step 1: Define Your Goals
What do you want PR to help you accomplish in the next 6–12 months?

Select all that apply.
- Media coverage (earned press)
- Podcast interviews
- Speaking engagements
- Book or product launch visibility
- Thought leadership positioning
- Crisis communications
- Event PR (launch, gala, campaign)
- Social or digital reputation support
- Influencer or brand partnership visibility

Step 2: Identify Your Assets

Before you spend, check what you already have (and what you'll need to build):

Asset	Do you have it?	Cost to develop (if needed)
Updated brand bio	Yes / No	$_____
Professional headshots	Yes / No	$_____
Media kit or one-sheet	Yes / No	$_____
Website/ landing page	Yes / No	$_____
Press clips or testimonials	Yes / No	$_____
Social profiles (aligned)	Yes / No	$_____

Step 3: Estimate Your Monthly PR Budget

PR Element	DIY / Agency	Estimated Monthly Cost
Strategy & Positioning	[ ] DIY [ ] Hire	$_____
Media Pitching & Follow-Up	[ ] DIY [ ] Hire	$_____
Podcast Outreach & Booking	[ ] DIY [ ] Hire	$_____
Media Training / Interview Prep	[ ] DIY [ ] Hire	$_____
Event PR Support	[ ] DIY [ ] Hire	$_____
Social/Digital Reputation Support	[ ] DIY [ ] Hire	$_____

Total Monthly PR Investment: $_____

Suggested Commitment Timeline: ___ months

Notes for Founders + Experts:

Real PR results typically take **3–6 months minimum** to gain traction

Investing in **positioning first** will save you money down the line

If you can't afford a full-service firm yet, start with:

- A strategy session
- A done-for-you media kit
- A podcast placement package

Spin. Scandal. Strategy. What really drives reputation?

Public relations often gets a bad rap, and this book aims to set the record straight.

In The Great PR Heist, strategist and media expert Adrienne Alexander unpacks how public perception stole the truth about Public Relations by distorting and manipulating the very people who benefit from it.

Part myth-buster, part industry blueprint, this book delves into the strategies behind effective PR and how to protect your brand from being lost in the noise.

Whether you're a founder, thought leader, or publicist in the trenches, this isn't theory; it's the playbook.

Adrienne Alexander is a seasoned public relations strategist, media expert, and certified conflict resolution specialist with over 23 years of experience helping brands, thought leaders, and changemakers amplify their voices.

Learn more at www.adriennedalexander.com

www.ingramcontent.com/pod-product-compliance
Lightning Source LLC
Chambersburg PA
CBHW052130030426
42337CB00028B/5106

9 7 8 9 8 8 4 6 2 0 5 7